MW01284726

1

For more information on the author, her services and events; please visit sheilahill.ca

Forward

I wrote this book because people need to be reminded that we are all in this together. Learning and growing and figuring out our 'stuff'.

Essentially we are all on a journey to becoming who we are meant to be all along.

As a Life Coach and Spiritual Guide I work with people every day who are striving to do more than just survive; they are looking to THRIVE in their lives.

Often the difference between SURVIVING and THRIVING are just some SHIFTS in perspective.

This book is a collection of concepts and ideas about how to live your life authentically, bravely and in a way that nurtures your soul. The ideas and perspectives are meant to be the "aha" moments that take hold and affect how you live your day to day life.

By putting these shifts into action you'll find clarity, peace, empowerment and fulfillment. You'll find the courage to step into your power, exercise your unique gifts and truly THRIVE in your life.

Keep this book in your bathroom or carry it in your purse or briefcase; the content is easy to read and doesn't require much time.

The chapters are short and the SHIFTING potential is impactful. You don't even have to read the book in order.

It will be as though I am right there with you, reminding you to "WAKE UP and SHIFT" so that you can live a BEAUTIFUL LIFE !

This book is dedicated to every; Guru, Coach, Author and Client who has contributed so profoundly to my own life's journey.

and

To my children, who are willingly and lovingly along for the ride.

Without every one of you, none of what is now my own Beautiful Life would have been possible.

Where the SHIFTs are Happening

<u>Self Care is **NOT** Selfish</u>

Self Care is a word that is used a lot more often than it is done. We are taught from a young age that looking after ourselves is secondary to 'being nice'. That meeting the needs of others must come first which often results in us losing our ability to nurture ourselves in a way that is meaningful and supportive of how we want to live.

Society expects us to always put others first and if you don't – well, you are being SELFISH.

It has taken me a long time to come to a clear understanding of what true Self Care is. Like so many other amazing life changing tools; Self Care is a practice. So start now and understand that:

TAKING CARE OF YOU IS YOUR JOB!

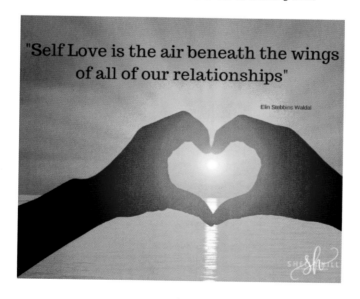

Embrace it as a necessity NOT a luxury.

What is *Self Care*?

I believe for many people, *Self Care* is all about 'looking after' yourself. Makes sense right? If I asked a bunch of random people on the street what they thought Self Care was (and I didn't by the way) they would say things like; going for a massage, watching my favorite show on TV, going for a run or a work out at the gym, having a long candle lit bath, getting a manicure or pedicure, going out for dinner with friends, or indulging in your favorite desert.

Does any of this resonate with you? As you were reading were you thinking – 'yep' , 'yep', 'yep', SEE ! I do self care (big smile, pat on the back.)

Those examples; although are all very nice things to do, are examples of "living". You should do that stuff regardless; do ALL of it, and the other stuff that I didn't mention.

It's called "living".

***Self Care* is not *selfish*; It is the opposite, it's self-full.**

It's about bringing the very best version of you to YOUR life!

Let me explain what life looks like when you don't make *Self Care* a part of your regular routine:

You are always rushing, feeling stressed and showing up in the lives of the people you love as a; cranky, impatient, tired, scattered version of you.

Your feelings are then worsened by guilt because you WISH; *"For The Love of God"* that you could just be nice, patient and loving. You are susceptible to catching colds, you are people pleasing everyone but yourself, you are saying 'yes' to events, and activities when you don't really want to do. You have a 'to do' list that never seems to end and that makes you feel like you never get anything accomplished.

You have bought into the idea that life is hard and that, true connection with yourself and with the people that you love is either rare or for others.

Does this sound like you?

How did I know? Because I have been there and know intimately the price that is paid for not practicing *Self Care*.

Here are some examples of what *Self Care* might look like if you were looking to be more present in your life, raise your self esteem and show up in the lives of those that matter as your true loving, patient, happy self.

1. **Learn to say NO.** If you are asked to do something or be somewhere that really just doesn't feel like a resounding YES.... Then it is a NO. A polite "I am sorry, but that isn't going to

work for me.." or, simply just "NO".
After all, "NO" is a complete sentence.

2. **Learn to meditate.** It is as easy as sitting still, closing your eyes, listening to something calming and concentrating on your breathing for 10mins every day.
(you might want to get more technical later, but for now – it's that simple). This will give your conscious mind a break as you become an observer of your thoughts, allow your cortisol levels to drop and give the little voice inside of you (your soul) to be heard.
(find my meditations at www.sheilahill.ca)

3. **Speak kindly to and about yourself.** Negative self talk lowers your confidence and programs low self esteem into your very being. If you say things about yourself like:

"I am such an idiot, I forgot (insert) again!".
"I am so (insert derogatory adjective)"
"I am a bad mom/wife/friend for yelling/forgetting/not listening" **STOP!!.**
Pretend you are speaking to a toddler who is learning to walk for the first time – think of how patient, understanding and encouraging you'd be and BE that for YOU.

4. **Just 'BE'.** You are a human BEING after all. NOT a human-doing. This one was hard for me to master but is absolutely the gateway to being fully present to see and experience the magic all around me. Try not to fill every minute of every day with 'stuff' that NEEDS to be done. Think about each item and access if it will really matter a year from now. Be conscious of what you allow to fill your time and what you are giving up by not being fully rested, calm and present.

5. **Be your own best friend.** You know what you'd do for a friend who was sick, having a bad day or maybe you just wanted her to know that you love him/her being in your life. Be that. Be the recipient of all the love, kindness and respect you'd give that special friend. Buy yourself flowers, take yourself to lunch with a good book, go for a long walk in nature, call in sick and have a 'me' day.

6. **Allow your inner child out to play.** Deep inside of each and every one of us is a child that loves to play. When did you last let your own inner child out? When did you last sing, dance, twirl, laugh, roll around on the floor with your pets, kids, spouse. Allow yourself to be silly and carefree? Tap back into the creative place in your heart that is longing for attention.

The next time you feel like life is getting off track, your relationships are out of whack, you are feeling 'off' or that the proverbial 'tail is wagging the dog'... stop and think:

"What have my *Self Care* practices been like lately?"

Acknowledge the answer, take a deep breath, be kind to yourself for falling off the wagon and get back on.

Now go love the crap out of yourself – EVERYONE will benefit!

See the back of this book for a **FREE 14 Day SELF LOVE Challenge.** I suggest you share it with a friend and do it together. Be accountable to one another and learn and support one another as you explore the practice of Self Care.

My Self Care Practice

Now that you have a clear idea of what Self Care is all about and you understand the importance of it; I'd like you to jot down some of the Self Care ideas you have that would be meaningful to you.

My daily Self Care practice will consist of :

_____

_____

_____

_____

_____

_____

_____

My weekly Self Care practice will consist of :

_____

_____

_____

_____

_____

_____

_____

When I recognize that I am showing up in a way that I am NOT proud of and I need a quick fix I will :

_____

_____

_____

_____

_____

_____

_____

_____

These are some other ways I can practice Self Care:

_____

_____

_____

_____

_____

_____

_____

People Pleaser Rehab

Are you a **People Pleaser?**

I don't mean, "Are you nice"

I mean do you find yourself constantly doing things for other people and coming up short in your own life because of it? Constantly seeking love, friendship, and validation from others?

Possibly even thinking "If I do this for them...they'll really like me, approve of me, validate me, make me feel worthy"?

I was a chronic **People Pleaser** until about 7 years ago when I realized how sick it was making me. Yes! physically, emotionally and spiritual sick!

You see, **People Pleasers** engage in pleasing behaviours in order to seek outward validation, love and a sense of worthiness. That was exactly how I used to live my life. I had no idea who I was, what my purpose was, how to self soothe or even love myself. I looked for it all from outsiders by over extending myself at every opportunity hoping and praying that someone would see me, love me or validate my existence in some way.

It was empty, incredibly subjective and soul sucking,

Being a chronic **People Pleaser** is not only detrimental to the pleaser's own life but can often have a huge effect on the lives of the people they 'help'. It can often lead to co-dependency and enabling – a self fulfilling prophecy.

People Pleasers ONLY attract Takers!

If you have read this far and are thinking that you might be in need of some REHAB; here are some tips you can start implementing right away that will take you away from People Pleasing and closer to self established self worth and self love:

1. **Learn how to say NO.** In actuality NO is a complete sentence on its own, but can feel kind of harsh at first so feel free to soften it. Your version could be "I am sorry but that won't work for me/ my schedule etc ". A full blown explanation is not needed and actually just reeks of 'please don't hate me'. Like a

muscle, learning how to comfortably say No takes practice and time – so go easy and start small.

2. **Pause.** Buy yourself some time with a pause. Remember your knee-jerk reaction is to always say YES, so by initiating a pause you are buying time to formulate a response that is more in alignment with what you want and need. The length of pause could range from a few seconds (while you check in) to a few days, depending on the ask. Take whatever time you need in order to feel good about your response.

3. **Limit your YES.** If you still feel that it is something you want to do then perhaps putting some healthy boundaries around the YES is what is required. Like setting an amount of time you are willing to give or only drive one way not both... be creative about the ways that you can still show up for people but that don't leave you depleted.

4. **Be willing to let relationships die.** As you rehabilitate yourself out of your people pleasing ways you may find that some relationships were dependent upon it. Be willing to let those relationships die... they weren't real anyway.

5. **Understand that you can't and shouldn't be everything to everyone.** Everyone has their own lessons to learn and by people pleasing and often rescuing people from their situations you are preventing them from learning how resilient, talented or creative they can be. This one comes up a lot in parenting. We all want our children to have

it all, have it easier than we did but pleasing them all the time is actually doing them a dis-service.

Rome apparently wasn't built in a day and re-training yourself out of being a People Pleaser won't happen over night either. Just bring awareness to when you are doing it, with whom you are most likely to do it and why. Then start little by little changing how you show up. As you go, you'll find that you have more time, more peace and clarity in your head and more space on your calendar.

Then you can use all that new found time, space and freedom to engage in Self Care practices that will help you find your validation, confidence and love from within.

<u>Numb and Neutral are NOT the Same!</u>

After growing up in a very turbulent household; witnessing and experiencing what would now be considered abuse most of my life, then suffering from post partum depression which gradually rolled into anxiety and panic disorder. I, myself used many forms of numbing in order to prevent me from feeling my life. Once I was awakened and I began to undo all the 'stuff', I got off all of the medications and then over time learned how to be more neutral and less numb.

Trust me, NUMB and NEUTRAL are not the same....

We all have 'something' that we do that takes the edge off. To help us get a reprieve, a breather, a momentary vacation from our crazy, stressed, over stimulated, over judged lives.

For some people it's smoking, for some it's drinking, or eating. Some people escape into sleep, their phone, video games or even exercise. Yes the 'vices' that people use go from the obvious to the not so much.

Every time something is used to take your focus and attention further away from being present and in the moment, you are **NUMBING**.

We NUMB to not have to 'feel'. When we don't like how our life feels and we engage in activities that takes our focus away from the 'pain' we are NUMBING.

The thing is that NUMBING doesn't just hold only the negative feelings, thoughts and experiences at bay – it holds *EVERYTHING* at bay.

Even the emotions we wish to experience, like: LOVE, JOY, and HAPPINESS.

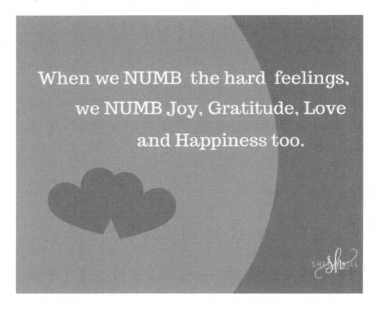

When we NUMB the hard feelings, we NUMB Joy, Gratitude, Love and Happiness too.

NUMB is; well…. NUMB

NEUTRAL on the other hand is a much healthier way to handle life. Being able to operate from a place of neutrality is EMPOWERING.

It says; "I allow in what serves me and what does not; I choose to let it wash away. I am in control of my emotions and responses to people and events.

I allow in LOVE, JOY, and HAPPINESS."

Being NEUTRAL is tapping into your inner wisdom, not being easily triggered into emotions that take you away from LOVE, JOY and HAPPINESS.

It doesn't mean that you aren't compassionate, or helpful or caring and kind; it means that you understand from a deeper place that everyone is on their own journey.

THAT NOT EVERYTHING IS ABOUT YOU.

How do I get from **NUMB** to **NEUTRAL** you ask?

Well, it too is a journey. A healing journey where you heal from your past to get rid of the triggers that caused you to move away from NEUTRAL in the first place.

It is a process of un-doing, purging, healing and re-framing so that **NEUTRAL** is all that is left.

Think about how your life 'feels' right now and get tuned in to where you are Numbing when you could be Neutral instead.

On the next page I have included a worksheet. Make some notes while this concept is fresh in your mind.

Here are some of the NUMBING activities I am aware
that I use or do:

_____
_____
_____
_____
_____

Here are some of the triggers I know cause me to revert
to NUMBING:

_____
_____
_____
_____
_____

If I were to trade NUMBING in for NEUTRALITY my
life would feel different in the following ways:

_____
_____
_____
_____
_____
_____

Sticks and Stones.....

Remember the rhyme, "Sticks and stones may break my bones, but words will never hurt me"? What if I told you that words actually have more POWER than any stick OR stone?

Words are one of the most powerful tools humans have and we use them so carelessly sometimes.

"Running with proverbial scissors as we thoughtlessly think and speak words with wreckless gay abandon."

We speak words and we think words but how often are we as mindful about the specific words we choose as we would be running with a knife, or scissors?

Many of my clients suffer from low self esteem or 'not enough-ness' as I call it. And, I did too!

Or perhaps a more honest answer would be that I still wrestle with it from time to time. But one of the biggest 'aha' moments I had came from being really aware of what the words were that were constantly rattling around in my head.

That is why I am sharing this concept with you, hoping that you'll take it on board and start to be more mindful of the words you use on yourself and on those you love.

Shifting this perspective will have more IMPACT than you can imagine!

Take Care of how you speak to yourself, you are always listening...

The Human Mind:

Each and every moment of everyday (except when we are sleeping) our *conscious mind* is taking in billions of stimuli; scents, words, sounds, feelings and sights. It can only handle so much, so it filters and files most of what is not immediately needed away.

Our *unconscious mind* on the other hand, never sleeps. It is alert, and processing each and every stimuli we receive and the feeling we attach to it, 24hrs a day, 7 days a week. It has no filtering system and cannot discern between what is real and what is imaginary. Our unconscious mind is in essence, our hard drive.

Every time we think a thought or speak a word to ourselves or someone else we are in essence 'installing' it into our own unconscious mind AND that of the intended recipient. Because the unconscious mind can't discern

between REAL and IMAGINARY; it deems whatever you said to be true.

The other tricky thing about the power of the *unconscious mind* is that it does NOT understand negatives.

For example;

Envision yourself walking down a flight of stairs in a new pair of shoes and you are thinking "don't fall, don't fall, don't fall"... what your unconscious mind hears is: "fall, fall, fall" ...and sets about trying to make your desire to 'fall' your experience.

So now that you are up to speed on an important part of how the mind works, let's take a look at some common fax pas and how to fix them.

Do you remember a time where you might have said:

"I am feeling fat...ugh!"

"I just can't sleep at night, I've never been a good sleeper...."

"I am never going to be able to achieve my goal...."

"This is just too hard!"

"My family will never understand me..."

"I never finish anything...what's wrong with me?"

"I am NOT enough...."

Be honest. I said them all ... as a matter of fact for a good portion of my life this was the sound track!

KNOW THIS.... you are always creating your reality!

In the words of Ice Cube:

"Check Yourself before you Wreck Yourself"

Here's another great example of how we have control over our life experiences using the power of words. It was never made more clear to me than when I read "Untethered Soul" by Michael A Singer.

He speaks of having a best friend; she's always around, ALWAYS talking and she's a real "Debbie Downer". She is always pointing out to you when you make mistakes. Reminding you how not enough you are and what a bad mom/wife/sister/daughter/friend you are.
(dad/husband/son/friend – keeping it fair)

How long would you want to stay friends with someone like that? Not long right?

Now imagine that this so called best friend is really your own mind and that was the track it played. Bringing you down and keeping you further and further away from your fullest potential for happiness. You get to choose whether you listen, engage, believe or change the track all together.

So kick that 'best friend' to the curb and start a new sound track using positive words and see how your life changes.

Here are some handy ways to re-frame almost any thought so that you are empowered and working with the universe and your *unconscious mind* to create the life experiences you desire and deserve:

replace CAN'T with CHOOSE NOT TO

replace SHOULD with COULD

(Yes! Please stop "shoulding" all over yourself!!)

replace HAVE TO with CHOOSE TO or WANT TO

replace TRY with WILL

Keep your thoughts clean and positive and carefully choose your words. BOTH with yourself and with every single person you interact with.

Use words as a magical life changing tool. Use them to heal relationships with others, use them to show gratitude. Most of all use them to be kind to yourself .

Words are one of the most powerful tools we have and YOU have control over how you choose to use them!

Being Present

I was well into my healing journey before I really understood what BEING PRESENT meant. It is one of the biggest struggles of our human existence. We are always either revisiting (or sometimes wallowing in) our past, which at its worst shows up as victimhood, depression and hopelessness OR focusing (being anxious) on our future.

I have personally set up camp in both locations and then flitted from one to the other for most of my life.

And yet...

The magical gifts in life are ONLY found in the moments when we are fully PRESENT and in the NOW.

Stop looking back

You aren't going that way!

Here is the **TRUTH**, it's simple and may seem cliché: You can't do anything about your past, It happened. It may have been uncomfortable, disastrous, or even horrendous. BUT that point in time is gone. The very energy and synchronicity of time, place and players is gone forever.

LET IT GO!

Another **TRUTH** is projecting our focus into the future which is "story telling" or IMAGINARY. You have no way of knowing how something is going to turn out, unfold or present its self to you….. so stop making stuff up about it!

I know you are thinking that you DO know – that let's say for example; the family BBQ is going to be a fiasco because Uncle Joe always picks a fight with his brother Larry.

How do you 'know'? because you learned from your past?

And…..there it is folks… dragging up the past to create a story about the future that hasn't happened. Don't do that!

Do you know what we love most about our pets and little children?

They are **PRESENT**.

They love, experience, and witness the world around them totally from the present moment. We love their innocence, their loyalty, their simplicity… why does that life have to exist for only our pets and kids? It doesn't.

We were all born with the hard wiring for 'flight' or 'fight'. It's our caveman response. In our past when things happened to us (which really happened 'for' us, but that's another lesson for another day) that weren't pleasant, we were protected by this mechanism. We instinctively would either stay and 'fight' or 'flee' (flight).

We don't technically live under those conditions anymore and haven't for many generations BUT we still have that wiring and it's preventing us from Being Present for some of the not so nice stuff and thus creating a need for healing.

I propose to you this solution.. **BE PRESENT** for **EVERYTHING!** (yep, even the sh*t)

Now obviously being present for the good, magical, and amazing stuff is easy. Being Present for the bad, the sh*t, the extraordinary sh*t, the uncomfortable, the *'this just might kill me'*… is A LOT harder.

What you need to do is; see it coming or acknowledge that it's happening, take a deep breath, and choose to emotionally STAY.

Don't allow your natural instinct of seeking emotional refuge to drive the bus.

Cry, scream, swear (a lot), and hit pillows. Whatever you need to do, do it! There is no 'right way' only 'your way' so feel it all and don't 'should' on yourself about it. Feel the whole emotional spectrum of what you are experiencing. Let it come up into your physical body and let it flow OUT. Don't stuff it, ignore it, or deny that it's happening; that will only create a need for it to be 'healed' at some other date.

Make sure you understand that last tip:

That which you are NOT present for the first time will only require 'healing' at some later date.

If you aren't **PRESENT** for it when it happens, you'll drag it around with you allowing it to taint every experience and relationship in your life thereafter.

When you are present for the difficult stuff you are a **SURVIVOR**. You are NOT a victim.

The language feels so much better doesn't it? Once you've fully experienced and survived, that moment will never happen again. It can't get you later… you did it, you passed!!

Now move on, BE PRESENT and see what it has to bring.

Healing our Past because we weren't PRESENT the first time:

Everything I have written about so far is how to be present going forward. But what if you have stuff you weren't present for in your past?

We were never taught how to be present and self heal before. If you have something from your past that is preventing you from being fully present in your life today, you need to heal it.

One way is to journal. Start writing down everything you remember about that particular experience; your childhood, abuse, loss of a loved one, a rotten teacher, divorce, or betrayal and feel everything you need to feel, let it come up, acknowledge it, let it out and know that more than anything you are a **SURVIVOR** (you're here aren't you?).

Or seek the guidance of a coach to help you navigate the healing process. Coaches are not emotionally attached to the trigger or the outcome; we will always see you for your best, we have tools to aid the process and many of us have our own life experiences to draw upon. We can guide, support and hold space for you to heal.

We are all beautiful creatures having experiences of all kinds every single minute of every single day. It can't be all good or we'd never grow OR appreciate what we have. The bad doesn't need to define or imprison us either...

BE PRESENT....... it truly is the GREATEST GIFT!

Four Faces of FEAR

Fear truly is at the root of almost all of the world's problems. In my line of business I come across various 'flavors' of fear all the time. People stuck in all manner of ways in their lives, some even paralyzed by fear.

Getting clear on what the fear actually is; calling it out of the darkness into the light and then moving through it is the only way out.

Inhale *Courage* Exhale *Fear*

Here are the Four Faces of Fear as I see them:

Fear as Faith : Many people have hang ups and fears that go back to their religious beliefs or upbringing. This is always a tricky one to navigate as I always attempt to respect my client's faith choices BUT sometimes their

understandings of things require some poking at. I firmly believe that regardless of the religious frame work you use to get there, there really is only ONE "all being". And that being, whomever you call him/her/it does NOT want you to suffer in their name, sacrifice your life and happiness for them or fear their existence.
You are here to **THRIVE!**

Fear as Lack of Trust: This one is really common, when someone's fear is actually rooted in their ability to trust others. Often people fear that someone won't show up for them, respect them, tend to their needs, manipulate them or worse. The fact is that all of these outcomes are possible and the undoing of the fear lies within. The trust must come from the person who has the fear. They need to learn to trust themselves enough to know that IF/WHEN they are in a situation where someone may take advantage of them that they **TRUST** themselves enough to stand up, speak up or walk away. We have NO control over what others do, we can only control our own response. **TRUST YOURSELF!**

Fear as Anxiety: Many people live in a state of constant fear. They are often paralyzed by it. Constantly afraid that they are not; good enough, smart enough, capable enough or resourceful enough. When fear is induced by anxiety the person is projecting into the future... they aren't being present. The future is unknown and often mostly unpredictable so anything the person in fear is telling themselves is really just a made up 'story'. By practicing BEING PRESENT they can start to alleviate their fear.

Fear that isn't yours: The world is in a state of fear. Watch the news, read a newspaper or any other media source and you'll find messaging of fear at every turn. When we are exposed to this kind of messaging it triggers us... makes us consider all the 'what ifs' as though they are real:

"What if that happened to me?"
"What if I am not safe?"
"What if my children are at risk?"

and so on. When we have family members who live in a constant state of fear the outcome is similar. We end up on their fear train and before we know it; it's left the station.

When we experience fear the best way to handle it is to become an observer of the situation. Then get clear on which of the four faces the fear is wearing and call it out.

Ask yourself is it real? Is it programming? Is it even yours?

Stop Saying You're Sorry!

Canadian's are known all over the world for our innate ability to always be polite. I am here to tell you that we've taken the "I'm Sorry" stuff more than a little too far.

Here is how this revelation came to me and with a little self awareness, it has changed how I interact with people in a BIG way.

I way lying awake in the middle of the night at the bedside of my son who had been admitted to hospital.

People say "I'm sorry" WAAAAY too much!

He had needed an IV line earlier that day and the nurse profusely apologized the entire time she was doing it and then apologized at the end and then again one more time as she passed by our cubical half an hour later.

I know in her heart she was sincerely 'SORRY' for any pain or discomfort she had caused but when I reflected back on the event I realized that the *energy* of the interaction was possibly more damaging than the event its self.

Allow me to explain:

When you say *"I'm sorry"* the energy of those words and the feeling that is expressed is that you are BAD, it has a negative energetic impact on your self esteem.

39

The number of times that lovely nurse said 'I'm sorry'; she may as well have been saying: "I am BAD, I am BAD, I am BAD". Which absolutely was not the case.

The fact that she works as an IV nurse in pediatrics probably means she says "I am sorry" ALL the time.

At the receiving end of all those *"I'm sorry's"* are children who are then victimized; NOT by the event but by the words of the interaction.

 It deems them powerless, makes them the victim of something negative. Something was done **TO** them.

Here's what I want you to learn from this concept:

What if we took the interaction and changed the *intention* of it?

What if the nurse said **"Thank you"** INSTEAD of "I'm Sorry" ?

"Thank You for being brave", "Thank You for being patient", "Thank You for co operating with me".

How much more **empowering** would that feel to the child? It would make them feel like they were doing something good. Participating on some level, rather than feeling like a victim and out of control.

How much better would the nurse feel every day being in the attitude of gratitude?

I am not saying that people shouldn't say "I'm sorry" anymore, just say it when it genuinely applies to the circumstance.

is the new I'm Sorry...

Otherwise challenge yourself to replace a knee jerk "I'm sorry" with **"Thank you".**

So the next time you are running late to meet a friend for coffee; instead of saying "I'm sorry I'm late", say "Thank you for waiting"

Thank you for being patient.
Thank you for understanding my circumstances.
Thank you for giving me space to figure myself out.
Thank you for supporting me.

There are millions of ways to make "Thank you" the new "I'm Sorry" changing that one small thing, those two little words will leave both people feeling empowered and in gratitude.

<u>OVER Independence, Is That a Thing?</u>

Is there actually such a thing as 'Over Independence'?

I mean we are taught through our formative years to 'do it ourselves', to 'learn'... in fact most of our life's journey is about becoming the ultimate in achievement – INDEPENDENT!

Those of us who have raised, or are raising children do so in hopes that one day they will be INDEPENDENT.

Able to sustain themselves on every level on their own.

Is it possible that there could be a downside to this push for independence?

Well there is. One of the cornerstones of the human condition is that we require connection. It's not a 'nice to have' it's necessary for our emotional, psychological and spiritual health. We crave; a sense of community, companionship, love and understanding from others.

We are very INTER-DEPENDENT beings.

This concept came to my attention while reflecting on how I was *feeling* living my life. Not how I thought it was...but how it actually feels. The answer that came bubbling to the surface (and not so gentle in its approach) was that I am lonely.

I have actually taken the spirit of INDEPENDENCE too far!

I am a single mom and independence is a requirement when you find yourself on your own and out numbered. At first it was a challenge for me, almost a game; put up Christmas lights on my own (check), did all the lawn care for a season (check), first trip to the hospital with a child alone (check), took the kids on a vacation alone (check), replaced the kitchen faucet (check), paid the bills, juggled the balls, made the meals, nurtured, coached and loved (check, check, check).

There is/was a period of empowerment that came from digging deep into my independence. I think a lot of single mom's probably have the same feeling:

'Been there, done that, proved my point;now where are the people?'

Sometimes all you
need is
a hand to hold
and a heart to listen

And not to dis-include other demographics who have the serious potential of taking INDEPENDENCE too far. Entrepreneurs; for example are another obvious group (of which I also belong....sigh).

So what to do about it?

Take off your suit of armour; your INDEPENDENCE SUPER SUIT and ASK FOR HELP!

INVITE PEOPLE IN!

Don't judge how they show up; if it's done 'right' or how you would have done it. Just be grateful that they chose you, they showed up when you opened yourself up and invited them in.
Ask a friend to lend an ear when you are having a bad day, ask for help to move that piece of furniture, ask for support, guidance and recommendations from friends, loved ones, your angels/guides. ASK. Be brave, be vulnerable and LET PEOPLE IN.

We all know how good it feels to be kind, helpful or offer assistance to others. Who are you to take that away from those who love you?

If you have taken INDEPENDENCE too far and find yourself lonely, secluded and your 'I can do it myself ' attitude a little tarnished and worn out. Start looking for opportunities to invite people in....often the most magical connections come from the most unexpected places.

Permission to be Grumpy

While on my journey to heal my life I read a lot of books, listened to speakers, watched YouTube videos and subsequently really took on board that being positive was where it was at. For a long time, I thought that that was the ONLY place I could be IF I truly wanted to heal, love, grow and find fulfillment in my life.

Boy did I have it wrong!

You only need to scroll down the news feed of any social media site to be inundated with positivity. Cute little memes that are meant to brighten your day. Inspirational quotes of courage, bravery, humor and encouragement....

Don't get me wrong, I do it too; sprinkling my positive vibe out into the world hoping that I am having a positive effect on someone's day. And I probably am.. and so are you.

After all; preaching, sprinkling and shouting positivity from the roof tops is SUPER trendy!

So, what if you are genuinely having a bad day?

What if, it feels like life has handed you a big 'ole bowl of crap?

What if you've been hurt, betrayed or dishonored in some way?

Are you supposed to slap a smile on your face and say **"Thank you"** to the universe for this incredible new learning opportunity? NO!

After all you are only human.

You see the thing about being human is that we are expected to experience the full range of emotions, the good ones and the *'bad'* ones.

In fact it is a requirement. We are supposed to fall down, so we can learn how to get back up. We are supposed to experience heart break so we will truly know how to experience love. We are meant to experience grief so we will know how to live.

Being positive ALL the time is A LOT of pressure!

Being positive all the time just isn't realistic. Sometimes you just need to embrace the mess that you are or the anger you feel and learn NOT to judge yourself so harshly for it.

It's easy to navigate the 'good' feelings with a positive mindset and share the 'vibe' with others in hopes of lifting the spirits of the world.

We all need to make an effort to not dwell in the negative but sometimes... we just need permission to be Grumpy.

And this is yours.

A Constipated Life

In my view we live a 'constipated' life, seldom able to 'flow' or be creative about our responses to people and experiences.

Allow me to explain with this analogy:

Have you ever filled a sponge with water until it was fully saturated? And then tried to add more water to it? What happens...it just runs off right?

In my view our lives are very similar to a sponge, we are FULL of; expectations, requirements, data and stimuli.

So full that we have to turn the radio down to think when we are driving! (yeah.. me too)

Using the same analogy this is how I see life. We are all sponges, chocked full of 'stuff' and I believe that the 'run off' could very well be; JOY, LOVE, FUN and ADVENTURE. The very experiences that we desire from life and are not able to grasp because our energy, our space and very existence is ...well.... CONSTIPATED. (nothing in/nothing out)

I facilitate a small group workshop called "Who Am I?" and in that workshop, one of the big topics is about "Making Space".

The subject we originally discussed as a group was the benefits of journaling and letter writing for self growth and healing but what it really is about is MAKING SPACE.

You see, the energy of every word, thought and emotion we have ever had or received lives within your body. We need to release it in order to rid ourselves of it so that we can MAKE SPACE for more. Our calendars are full, our heads are full, our bodies are full of toxins and stress, our relationships are sometimes 'full' (of friction and misunderstanding) .

We are SO full that we are unable to think clearly, show up authentically, be creative about our lives, and give and receive LOVE....

If you feel like you are on the treadmill of life, that your relationships are stale and perhaps, so are you... MAKING SPACE is the answer and here are some suggestions on how to do it:

1. **Journaling** – stay in touch with your inner voice through journaling. Write about your day, clear your head of all the chatter simply acknowledge and release it. No judgment. MAKE SPACE!

2. **Letter Writing** – this isn't the kind of letter that goes anywhere – it's for you. Look into your past and know that the energy of disappointment, heartache, trauma and fear is still living within you unless you've done something to release it. Write a letter to your childhood self, write a letter to your parent, write a letter to anyone whom you have 'stuff' trapped inside about and don't give them the letter just know that the work needing to be done is done. MAKE SPACE!'

3. **Spend time alone** – just being with yourself without other people and all their expectations around you. Be an observer of your thoughts. Acknowledge what it feels like to be away from the major players in your life (your spouse, your kids etc). Look at them from a different vantage point. Use your imagination and explore what it's like to be them. ("absence makes the heart grow fonder"). Explore who you are being and what if anything you'd like to change. Take time away. MAKE SPACE!

4. **Laugh** – having fun and being silly is a huge release of energy. Laughter and Love are of the highest vibrational frequencies and bring with it physical, emotional and spiritual benefits. Nothing like a laugh until you pee to clear out the old and make room for new. It's fun to MAKE SPACE!

5. **Cry** – crying isn't an indication of something that needs healing, it IS healing. You don't need to know why or analyze and judge the crap out of yourself over it. If you feel like you need to cry, then cry. It clears out the energy closets. Clears your emotional being and your head. Grab a box of tissues and MAKE SPACE!

6. **Travel** – whether you go for a long drive in the country or half way across the world. Travel is a great way to disconnect from your day to day life and responsibilities. It refuels your soul and allows for a different perspective upon your return. Seeing, being and experiencing your life from a totally different place is invigorating. It may challenge your belief system and your way of being as you are exposed to differences in nature, people and cultures. You grow and you learn. You MAKE SPACE for something new.

51

There are lots of ways to MAKE SPACE. Find what works for you and give yourself a gift, I assure you that it WILL allow for more **JOY, LOVE, FUN** and **ADVENTURE** to show up in your life.

Dealing with Other Peoples 'Stuff'? – Be a Tree!

When faced with other people's stuff do you react like a FLAG or a TREE?

Each and every one of us are affected by the things that others do, or say or how they act. Most often when it's someone we are in a more intimate relationship with; our spouse, boss, mother, sibling or child we are **MORE** affected by their state of being.

Think of a situation when your boss, spouse or child were in a bad mood about something. Acting out of their own pain, frustration or discomfort...how did that affect you?

When we allow another person's frame of mind; the things they say that are unkind or intolerant, or their general mood to affect us – we are being a **FLAG**.

As a Flag we live our lives; more or less grounded in who we are and know that what we are doing, thinking or saying is 'mostly' who we want to be. As a FLAG, it's only when the '*weather conditions*' are ideal that we are able to maintain our sense of peace and calm.

When the WIND from another person's state of mind that doesn't match ours comes blowing in... we flap in the storm. Wondering what we could have done differently, what we did wrong, what we need to do to ease the other persons discomfort. We jump to attention, into *'rescue'* mode to try and save them. But mostly, if we are honest; we are really trying to save ourselves from their *'wrath'*.

The thing is, that usually NONE of the other person's state of mind has anything to do with us. They are acting out of their own pain, frustration or discomfort and we, are being a **FLAG.** When being a **TREE** would be better for us and all the same to them anyway. (and likely better for them too).

So what if you could be a **TREE?**

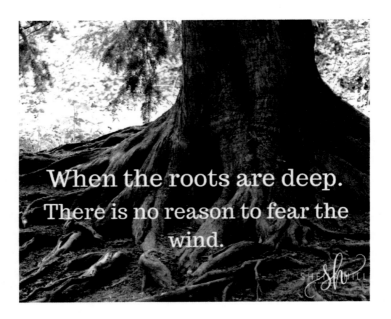

When the roots are deep.
There is no reason to fear the wind.

Grounded, standing tall, knowing who you are, deeply rooted in your value and sense of worth.

Calm and confident. Allowing the WIND of other people's 'stuff' to simply blow through your branches?

Yes, your branches may bend a little depending the person or situation but unlike the **FLAG** your entire mood does NOT have to be affected. The situation does NOT have to leave you flapping in the wind struggling to regain your own sense of stability, calm and peace.

A **TREE** can provide empathy, compassion, understanding and patience WITHOUT weathering the storm.

The choice is easy: **BE A TREE!**

<u>Motivation vs. Inspiration</u>

Have you ever just NOT felt "motivated" to do something? Perhaps you are procrastinating or waiting for the exact RIGHT conditions to be in place for you to get moving on a project or idea.

Do you sometimes find that you are frustrated with yourself?

Here's why....

*There is a HUGE difference between being **MOTIVATED** to take action and being **INSPIRED** to.*

Being **MOTIVATED** comes from that EGO place of SHOULD.   It sounds like this:

"I should get (name task) done".

"If I get (name task) done I will look good/garner respect/feel loved by my family or colleagues".

"Once (name task) is done I will experience more .....happiness, abundance, health – whatever".

It's the "IF I DO, THEN I WILL HAVE, SO I CAN BE.."
trap.

It is a forced way of looking at an action and although it works sometimes, the same old routine of PUSHING yourself to stay motivated gets to be very tiring.

Being **INSPIRED** to do something comes from 'spirit', in fact that's the very origin of the word. (IN SPIRIT).

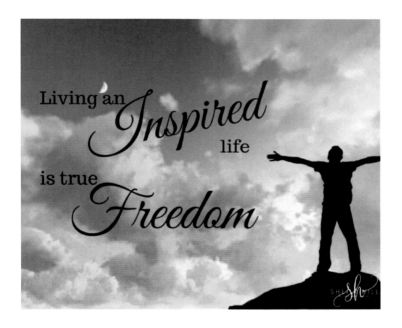

When something resonates with your very souls knowing; you feel INSPIRED, PASSIONATE, and EXCITED to get working on the task that INSPIRED you in the first place.

The ideas, creativity and solutions to problems flow easily. You feel 'in the zone'. You literally feel the proverbial wind at your back....

Take running as an example: for one person going for a run could represent honoring their body, connecting with nature, clearing their mind and feeling free.

For another person; they could not possibly come up with an activity they would rather do less!

The first person would feel INSPIRED to go for a run, the second would have trouble drumming up the MOTIVATION to go.

The first person would find time in their busy schedule, overcome perceived hurdles and obstacles and make a priority of 'doing what they love'. The second person would likely be beating themselves up with all the reasons why they 'should' go for a run and none of those reasons are very inspiring.

The point of this is to bring your attention to the difference between being MOTIVATED to act and being INSPIRED to.

When you are INSPIRED, you are in 'flow' with your own heart's desire (and thus with the universe), no matter what the task or activity is.

Do more of what you are INSPIRED to do and you'll find that Happiness, Peace and Fulfillment comes following closely behind.

Create Boundaries NOT Barriers

There is a palpable difference between having healthy **BOUNDARIES** and creating **BARRIERS** in our lives.

Boundaries are like a pre-set contract that you make with yourself and thus with the world around you. An *'offensive'* move in the game of life.

It's knowing yourself well; knowing your comfort zone, your triggers and the things, words and experiences that are absolute deal breakers.

Boundaries require really knowing yourself and being able to hold the world to the standard you set for how you want to experience your life.

For example:

A **Healthy Boundary** might be that you don't welcome house guests stay any more than 3-4 days. Perhaps you make this 'declaration' because you know that you love having family and friends visit but you also know that you aren't able to sustain the *'happy host/hostess'* hat for anything more than 3-4 days. At which point your level of enthusiasm isn't really beneficial to you or your guest.

This boundary is respectful to how you like to show up. It isn't dependent upon WHO the guest is or what the circumstances are around the planned visit. It just 'is'.

Another good example would be; working overtime. Perhaps your boundary is that you'll work overtime Monday thru Friday but not on the weekends. It's clear; it isn't subjective to the project, event, employer or any outlying circumstances. It just 'is'.

Barriers on the other hand are more of a *"defensive"* move. It's anxiety producing because it comes from a place of not knowing what is going to come at you next and when it shows up; you won't know what to do, say or how to react. So you flip into fight or flight mode and throw up a wall.

By putting up barriers you not only keep out the undesired; you keep out Joy, Adventure and Love.

Barriers are a prison you create for yourself.....

Healthy boundaries set you FREE!

People tend to put up barriers when they aren't clear on who they are and what makes them most fulfilled.

Often these people think that being a doormat means being 'nice'. They are chronic 'people pleasers' (been there and designed the T-shirt!).

Barriers go up when your sister-in-law calls, because you know that she's going to ask to stay at your place while she is in town on business and you don't know how to handle it. Barriers go up when your boss walks into your office because you know that he's going to ask you to work overtime and you don't know what to say.

Barriers ruin relationships – period.

Boundaries honor relationships by honoring the person putting them in place. It allows them to be clear and concise with what 'works for them' and 'what doesn't' in a way that is NOT subject to the person or situation at hand.

Practice creating and communicating Healthy Boundaries. Bring awareness to what and who leaves you feeling dishonored and make a 'plan' .

Tear down the barriers, they aren't keeping you safe – they are keeping life out!

<u>You Have a Super Power!</u>

Did you know that you have a 'super power'?

YOU DO!

And not just because you are special (well, you are) but it's something everyone has: their INTUITION.

It's a 'gut' feeling, a 'sixth sense', a "knowing" without knowing how you know.

What keeps many people from being able to tap into their own innate 'Super Power' is their EGO.

The "Ego" is the image we have of ourselves through the eyes of the world around us, it's how we show up in our lives. It's all the labels we identify with, our personality and our judgment of ourselves and others.

The 'Ego' was created to keep us safe. To alert us of danger, to keep us small so that everything would be predictable. The fact that it exists is hugely necessary in human existence AND so is knowing when and how to politely thank it for its opinion and tell it to 'shut up'.

Here's how to tell when your Ego is in charge:

- You find yourself consumed by emotion; usually more negative emotions such as: jealousy, shame, guilt, anger and fear.

- You identify your 'worth' with external material things like a big house, a 'good' job, a certain body type/weight.
- You always look for validation from others.
- Your inner dialogue is strife with anxiety inducing words of "not enough", "not worthy" etc
- You express anger, resentment, jealousy and frustration.

When you realize your Ego is running the show know that you don't HAVE to listen to it. It isn't necessarily the REAL you. Become an observer of the Ego; thank it, forgive it and delve into connecting with your soul.

Your soul IS your truest authentic self.

Here's how to recognize your Soul:

- You feel and experience positive emotions such as; love, joy, peace, and compassion more often.
- It guides you with 'gut feelings' and 'hunches' that you can't explain.
- You are able to love and accept yourself unconditionally, regardless of your status, material inventory or historical experiences.
- You are forgiving of others and can more easily accept other people as they are without judgment.
- You have dreams and desires but your self-worth is not attached to them or their ultimate outcome.

The beauty of the human experience is that you get to live life connected to both your Ego and your Soul. You get to decide in any given situation on any given day WHO gets to drive the bus.

Your relationship with your Ego is likely very strong and well established. With self awareness you will learn to recognize from which place you are operating and will be able to make adjustments accordingly.

If you are looking for ways to strengthen your relationship with your Soul; connect with your inner guidance through activities like meditation, spending time in nature, journaling, and being creative.

Exercise your SUPER POWER everyday and see how BALANCED you become.

Discover how much more at peace you are when your EGO isn't telling you all day long that you are 'not enough'. Find your self-confidence, grow and all of your relationships deepen.

There is literally NO downside from learning how to tap into your innate Super Power.

Forgiveness ..Who Is It REALLY For?

YOU that's who !

Lack of Forgiveness is one of the leading causes for being 'stuck' and YOU have the power to unstick yourself .

Self forgiveness is the key, regardless of who did what to whom.

In the most common and traditional sense, forgiveness occurs when a persecutor does a 'bad' – apologizes to the victim and the victim forgives the persecutor.

Often the role the victim played has to be forgiven first and it usually is that he or she gave away their power....

Here's a common example I see in my coaching practice:

John and Jane are married. John has an affair and subsequently they get divorced. (Now, before you lose your hat... I fully realize that this scenario could have easily gone down the other way around – this is just an example).

Now Jane is feeling; hurt, angry and betrayed.

Traditional wisdom would say that Jane needs to forgive John so she can heal and move on with her life.

In actuality, the gift of *forgiveness* is something that Jane needs to give herself **FIRST!**

She may be angry, hurt and feel betrayed for what John did; but at her core, she is really disappointed in herself for being a *'fool'*.

She's judging herself for not noticing the signs, shaming herself for not being pretty enough, smart enough or good enough. Most of if not all of which is NOT true.

Jane needs to forgive herself for the part she played in this scenario, bring kindess and acceptance into her heart and stop the should of's, blaming

THAT is where the real healing comes from.

What about John? he needs to forgive himself too.

AND..... eventually Jane will need to forgive John; because the price for Jane to carry around anger, hurt and betrayal for the rest of her life is TOO HIGH.

People often get confused; FORGIVENESS isn't the same as OK-ness. It's NOT ok, you aren't condoning what the other person did – you are choosing to be FREE!

The need for self forgiveness is something that shows up in almost every relationship. Forgive yourself for not being the 'perfect' parent, forgive yourself for judging your own parents, forgive yourself for every time you didn't do the right thing, forgive yourself for not being enough for someone, doing enough, or saying enough. Just forgive yourself and be better the next time.

We all too often seek from others what we need in order to soothe our feelings, heal our hurt or pain;

FORGIVENESS is one of them.

Everything we *really* need is INSIDE of us already; including FORGIVENESS.

Forgiveness is a POWERFUL gift.... start with YOU!

ReCap.... Wait there is MORE!

Well if you've read the book in full to this point you've made some pretty incredible shifts towards living a Beautiful life! You've:

Started to **LOVE** yourself more...

You are no longer setting yourself on fire...

You are more **MINDFUL** of your words...

You are being more **PRESENT** more often...- even for the crappy stuff..

You are living less in fear and more often in **FAITH,** even if it's faith in yourself...

You are saying **THANK YOU** more often than I'm Sorry...

You are no longer doing the over independence thing and surrendering to your **INTERDEPENDENT** nature...

You understand that being **GRUMPY** is a requirement for being Human...

You've made **SPACE** in your life for Joy, Love and Adventure...

You are a **TREE**...

You are living a more **INSPIRED** life...

You know yourself better and therefore create
HEALTHY BOUNDARIES instead of barriers...

You recognize the voice of your Ego and tap into your
INTUITION more regularly...

You have fully **FORGIVEN** yourself for your past ...

**And now it's time to MANIFEST some MAGIC into your
life!**

MANIFESTING MAGIC

So I'll assume that you'd really like to MANIFEST some pretty awesome stuff in your life. Say a new car, a new job, a relationship, more money, better health? Yeah I thought so!

First I'd like to address the elephant in the room. Many of my clients have a 'story' attached to the desire to manifest awesome stuff. It usually goes back to either religion or worthiness. So let me be clear:

YOU ARE WORTHY OF DESIRING TO MANIFEST WHATEVER YOU WANT!

I mean anything and everything. We live in a world chock filled with abundance, we are here in human form to have fun, learn and experience to our hearts desire – in essence, life is supposed to be a 'play ground'. So drop the guilt and the self limiting beliefs and let's get your Manifesting Mojo revving into high gear!

Want to know the truth about MANIFESTING?

YOU ARE ALWAYS MANIFESTING!!!

YES, EVERY MINUTE OF EVERYDAY...THE GOOD STUFF, THE BAD STUFF AND THE IN BETWEEN....

You see the truth about Manifesting is that it's all about 'energy'. Every thought, emotion, belief, spoken word and action that you have is energy. Literally everything – even when you sleep. So you are always emitting a frequency of energy out into the world. It seeks a vibrational match and comes back to you in whatever form it matches with.

Let's look at a couple of examples...

What if you don't like your job and you want to find a new one. But your thoughts are something like this..." I hate this job, I NEED to find another one" now you are emitting the frequency of NEED and guess what you'll attract? Yes, more NEED into your life.

What if you are desperate to meet your sole mate? Perhaps you are on multiple dating sites and engaging in conversation with pretty much anyone who contacts you... hoping this is 'the one'? If you are 'desperate' to meet someone... you are going to end up attracting multiple forms of desperation into your life. Maybe even a 'desperate' partner.

Imagine if you shifted your energy, your thinking, and your beliefs.

What if you saw that job as a stepping stone for something new and amazing? And that while you are doing the appropriate action items you did so with excitement and creativity INSTEAD of need.

What if you truly loved yourself and enjoyed your own company... maybe even thought of yourself as pretty 'awesome'? Can you imagine what you would attract into your life if you tuned your Manifesting Mojo into the AWESOME channel?

By shifting YOUR energy you create a shift in the energy of your life.

Make decisions from a place of LOVE and attract more LOVE, belief that you are already living an ABUNDANT life and you'll attract more ABUNDANCE.

YOU ARE ALWAYS MANIFESTING... keep your thoughts, feelings, words, beliefs and patterns pointed in the direction of what you would LIKE!

Now here is the all important tip:

Don't Follow the Waitress into the Kitchen!

Allow me to explain. When you set an intention that you'd like to attract something or someone into your life you should do so with clarity and high vibing energy. The universe doesn't exactly speak English (or any other language for that matter) it speaks and understands your vibration (energy). So really being excited about what you are looking to manifest and truly believing at your core that it is on its way to you is **CRUCIAL!**

Place your 'order' and LET IT GO....allowing the 'how' and the 'when' to be completely out of your control. Understand that the universe knows more than you do about what is possible.

I'll use an example to make this part clear:

When you are at a restaurant with friends and you place your order for food with the waitress you simply place your order clearly and concisely and then resume your conversation. Deep down inside you have a 'knowing' that the food will come and when it does, it will be great. Right?

Manifesting is exactly the same. Place your order and then move on...

Imagine if you followed the waitress into the kitchen and 'supervised' as she placed your order with the cook, you reminded her over and over how you wanted it cooked and what garnishes to include and then you stood there and watched as the chef cooked the food. You would NEVER do that...

You would be offending the waitress and the chef, you'd be missing out on the fun at the table and slowing everyone down from being able to do their job.

When you desire to manifest something or someone into your life – don't lather it in doubt by looking for it every minute of the day, by placing the order over and over and questioning if anyone is actually listening or by trying to control to much of the process. Remember the universe speaks in the language of energetic vibration and DOUBT is one of the biggest BLOCKERS in the flow of energy.

 Place your 'order', have **FAITH**, let go of the 'how' and 'when'....and allow the magic to unfold!

Ok, so remember when I said that you are ALWAYS manifesting?

Every minute of every day... EVEN on the 'bad' days....

Did you panic a little? Did you have a moment when you remembered last Tuesday when you were in a foul mood and have suddenly realized that you were manifesting then too?

Well the Universe has a LAW in place that will save your butt from those kinds of days. It's called the LAW OF GESTATION. The Law of Gestation is the lag time between the 'seed' being planted and the 'crop' being ready to harvest (metaphorically speaking)

The Law of Gestation works off of your energetic vibration. When you are in lower vibration your ability to Manifest slows down and the time it takes for your Manifesting efforts to come to fruition is longer. It's the Universes way of saying "Are you sure?" .

This gives you time to; have happier thoughts, do better things, transform your way of being and generally raise your vibration. It literally 'saves' you from manifesting a whole bunch of unwanted crap into your life by slowing everything down. It allows you to get clear, work out your 'stuff' and be more purposeful about how you show

up in your life.

People who tend to vibe high most of the time; they are able to Manifests much quicker because they are *'more often'* clear and purposeful in their day to day, they love themselves and others, they are less judgmental and more open to being in the flow of life. They have less 'off' days and are therefore less likely to manifest what they don't want.

The Law of Gestation works in your favor. It allows you to be human; to have off days and then course correct.

Now make a list, set an intention, do a meditation or whatever other form of communication you'd like to use to send your desired wishes out into the universe and then LET IT GO!

14 DAY SELF LOVE CHALLENGE

Each of these Self LOVE activities will only take about 5-10 minutes to do. Most of them are completely FREE (monetarily speaking) and ALL of them will give you some really great examples of what SELF LOVE could look like when you infuse your life with it.

I recommend that you invite a friend to do the challenge with you; perhaps you'll get creative and carry on the LOVE with yourselves and each other after the challenge is over.

Welcome to DAY #1

Today is called **"Self Care is NOT Selfish"**.

So often people end up subscribing to the roles that are assigned them and the main one is "nurturer"... why is it then we are so horrible at nurturing ourselves?

At some point in time we were told that looking after yourself is SELFISH and I am here to tell you that it is one of the most important tools for allowing you to bring the best version of yourself to **YOUR** life.

You have already completed the first activity by reading the first chapter of this book. I want you to be really clear on what my 6 Self Care steps are so if you need a reminder; read chapter #1 again.

NOTE FROM THE COACH:
It's about time you jumped on board...you are worthy of Self Care without question! I am thrilled you are finally learning how to do it!!!!

Welcome to DAY #2

Today is called "**Mirror Mirror**"

How often do we as women avoid looking in the mirror? OR, when we do all we can see are the imperfections?

Today's activity is to spend **5 minutes** looking in the mirror in the spirit of LOVE.

Look deep into your eyes and say **"I LOVE YOU"**. Yes, it will feel; odd, strange, awkward or maybe even stupid…

Say "I LOVE YOU" to yourself over and over until the 'weird' feeling begins to ease or go away.

NOTE FROM THE COACH:
I LOVE YOU …even more on the days that you can't seem to find it for yourself.

<u>Welcome to DAY #3</u>

Today is called "**NO**"

Did you know that 'NO' is a complete sentence all on its own? Well it is.
Being able to say NO is an act of self love because it keeps you in *integrity* with yourself.

When we say 'YES' to things, activities, tasks and people that we really FEEL like it should be a "NO".....
we fall out of LOVE with ourselves.

Today's activity is to practice saying "NO" when you really feel that it should be.
The best way to do this is to PAUSE before responding and check-in with yourself... be honest and exercise your NO muscle.

Here are some things that I could learn to say NO to:

_____
_____
_____
_____
_____
_____
_____

NOTE FROM THE COACH:
When you say NO to something... you are REALLY making space or saying YES! to something or someone else. Work that muscle baby!

<u>Welcome to DAY #4</u>

Today is called "**Love Language**"

We are all hardwired to both give and receive love in a certain way. This is called our "Love Language". The key to being successful in LOVE, both with yourself and others is to understand what language you speak.

Today's Activity is to do the "5 Love Languages" quiz and reveal what your Love Language is. This will make learning how to SELF LOVE so much easier – because you'll have some insight into HOW you receive love.

Take it one step further and share your results with your significant other!

<u>www.5lovelanguages.com/profile</u>
(The 5 Love Languages by Gary Chapman)

My primary Love Language is: _____

My secondary Love Language is:_____

These are some examples of how I would like to receive love: _____
_____
_____

NOTES FROM THE COACH:
I LOVE YOU in all the languages; acts of service, gifts, quality time, words of affirmation, physical touch, Chinese, Russian, Spanish, sign language ....

Welcome to DAY #5

Today is called "**Fun with Food**"

So much of our time spent in the kitchen falls under the "HAVE TO" category.
It can sometimes lead to making us resentful and it affects our relationship with food.

Often we also get cornered into only cooking the foods the family like and our own tastes and desires continue to go unmet.

Today's activity is to have some fun with food.

Cook up your favorite recipe (yes, even if the kids won't eat it), bake something. If this totally doesn't sound like your thing... order in or go out.
But make it YOUR choice!

Even picking up your favorite pastry at the local bakery can feel like an indulgence.

NOTE FROM THE COACH:
The more you LOVE what you cook, LOVE what you eat and LOVE yourself for indulging in it... the less the number of calories. (..it's an energy thing)

<u>Welcome to DAY #6</u>

Today is called "**LOVE your 'flaws**"

We really are our own worst enemy when it comes to our perceived 'flaws'. We fixate on parts of our physical selves that we don't like while others see us as beautiful.

The truth is that if you have a wrinkle it proves you have "lived", if you have stretch marks your body has proven its self to you. If your stretch marks are from having children… you made a whole and real person!

Today's activity is to LOVE your 'flaws'.

Whether it's a wrinkle, a mole, a dark spot, stretch marks or cellulite.

CELEBRATE that you are alive.

Take 5 minutes and inventory your body with LOVE. Use a gentle finger or some cream and slowly and with intention caress each and every part of yourself that you perceive as flawed and tell it you love it.

For it is proof that YOU have lived, loved and made an impact on the world in your own unique way.

NOTE FROM THE COACH:
YOU are a freaking MIRACLE! There are NO extra peeps on the planet. I Love you for being here!

Welcome to DAY #7

Today is called "I AM___"

There is a powerful statement that says;
"Whatever follows "I AM" will be.."

If you follow "I AM" with hungry, you seem to get more hungry.
If you follow "I AM" with the word tired, you feel more tired.

The power of this concept has no limits. If you follow "I AM" with the words like sad, fat, broke or lonely…guess what? Yep – you experience more of it.

Today's activity is to create your own "I AM" statement (or as many of them as feels right to you). Type it up, print it and tape it somewhere you will see it often. (on your laptop, bathroom mirror or car dash).

Some example 'I AM" statements are:
 "I am enough", "I am worthy", "I am beautiful", "I am love", "I am abundant", "I am smart".

NOTE FROM THE COACH:
IF I were to create one for you, it would say "I am enough, worthy, beautiful, love, abundant, kind, happy, and creative"…. but that's just me. Love ya!

<u>Welcome to DAY #8</u>

Today is called "**Move and Breathe**"

So much of our time is spent being sedentary. We sit at work, we sit in our cars, in meetings etc.

The fact is that we are energetic 'beings' and energy NEEDs to move! In order to fully LOVE our lives and our bodies we need to nourish it with movement and breath, not just food and water.

Today's activity is to "Move and Breathe". Go for a walk, go to a yoga class, put on some fun music and dance in your underwear (ok, you can wear clothes too). Move your entire body doing something pleasurable.

Take deep breaths, we tend to only bring our breath in half way…breathe deeply. Allow your senses to be flooded with everything that surrounds you. The sounds, smells and sights.

Usher in JOY!

NOTE FROM THE COACH:
I am imagining you walking and breathing and dancing and smiling and filling your body with joy with each and every movement…. It looks soooo GOOD on you!

Welcome to DAY #9

Today is called **"Phone a Friend"**

Do you have a friend or family member that you have been 'meaning' to reconnect with and you JUST haven't made the time?

Has the time since your last connection gone so long that it is starting to feel awkward when you think about picking up the phone?

Do you long for the comfort, familiarity and joy that person brings to your life?

Today's activity is to make the time to reconnect with someone in your life that is important to you. Feeling connected to people outside of our immediate sphere of the day to day fills your heart with love and joy. Laughing with an old friend, recounting the latest and greatest with someone you feel close to is the best therapy.

Call your "person" and chat for hours OR call and just tell him/her that you LOVE them..... and watch how your heart sings!

NOTE FROM THE COACH:
(Ring Ring) Hello?.... you are totally ROCKING this Self Love challenge. Just wondering what parts of it you are going to stick with? All of it I hope.

Welcome to DAY #10

Today is called "**Blooms for You**"

Who doesn't love the freshness and color flowers brings to a space?
Who says you HAVE to wait for your significant other to buy them for you?

Romancing yourself through buying flowers is a huge act of worthiness. It says;

"I picked them, I like them and I bought them... why? because I am worth it!"

Today's activity is to buy yourself a bunch of flowers. You can go to a florist or stop at the local grocery store. Buy a bunch of flowers or a plant – whatever speaks to you. Go with the intention of treating yourself.

Pick what you LOVE, bring them home, put them in a vase and find a spot to put them that is in prominent plain sight. Every time you look at them you'll be reminded how much you LOVE you.

NOTE FROM THE COACH:
Beep, beep, beep, beep... that's the delivery truck backing up your driveway. I am having a truckload of flowers delivered to you – 'cause that's how much I LOVE YOU!

Welcome to DAY #11

Today is called "**Fancy Soap**"

The ritual of bathing can be about so much more than just getting clean. It's a time of the day when we are most intimate with ourselves. And yet it is most often a time when we are rushing to get ready to "be" somewhere or 'do' something for someone else.

How often do you bathe and look at your legs and think …" …can I get away with not shaving again? I just don't have time"? (yep..me too!)

Today's activity is to use the 'fancy soap'. Take a long hot bath, add candles, a glass of wine if you'd like.

But use the fancy soaps or body wash. Imagine as you soak in the tub with your thoughts how nice it feels to be indulging in YOU.

As you wash, wash away all the thoughts, emotions, and feelings that are yours or other peoples that don't bring you JOY.

Once you are done and dry and it's time to moisturize; imagine you are lathering on confidence, worthiness and self love . If having a bath just doesn't appeal to you… then have a long hot shower instead!

NOTE FROM THE COACH:

Rubba dub dub…there are 3 in my tub. ME, MYSELF and I and we all LOVE each other! You are really getting the hang of this aren't you?

Welcome to DAY #12

Today is called "**Just BE**"

Ahhh.. the art of being PRESENT. In a world that is full of stimulation and one that glorifies the idea of BUSY- it can be hard to learn how to just "BE".

Many of us don't know how to stop and even when we do the list of 'to do's' rattle around in our head and prevents us from truly being present in our lives.

Today's activity is to indulge in a little bit of 'just being' YOU. Set 30 minutes aside today where you can just be with yourself; no phone, laptop, Ipad, computer, kids or other perceived distractions.

Say to yourself:

"Whatever needs me can wait while I become a better version of myself. My lists can wait, the chores can wait, it WILL all wait for me and that is how beautiful my life is".

Now sit and stare out the window and allow your mind to wonder (observe and acknowledge where it goes), or sit with a journal and allow the words to flow first from your head and then from your heart onto the paper. If you find it too challenging then pick up a book or magazine and read for ONLY for pleasure.

NOTE FROM THE COACH:

The beauty of your inside is showing on the outside now that you are putting yourself first...and let me tell you 'You are looking marvelous D'harling"

Welcome to DAY #13

Today is called "**Meditation**"

The practice of Meditation is one that has so many benefits: Physically, Emotionally, Spiritually the list goes on and on. One of the biggest benefits is learning how to quiet the 'monkey' mind. This is the part of your brain that keeps you spinning, the constant chatter, and the string of thoughts that goes on and on . How many of those thoughts actually bring you JOY?

Today's activity is to practice the art of Meditation. Sit in your car, your bedroom, or a quiet spot in your office. Anywhere you can find to be comfortable and not distracted for 15 minutes. Click on the link below and allow my guided meditation to take you on a journey deep within yourself. Reconnecting you to YOU and filling you with Self Love.

www.sheilahill.ca/meditations

NOTE FROM THE COACH:

Did you know that 15mins of deep meditation is equivalent to 1 hr of sleep? Huh

Welcome to DAY #14

Today is called "**Love Letter**"

Congratulations for completing the first 13 days of the SELF LOVE challenge! This challenge has taken you on a little LOVE journey where you've been able to practice various forms of Self Love. Now it's time to bring it all together.

Today's activity is to write yourself a LOVE Letter.

Write a letter telling yourself all reasons you LOVE you! Inventory all the thoughts, emotions and feelings that have come up over the last 13 days and love yourself through them.

Be your own 'best friend'. Be compassionate, kind and encouraging.

Never underestimate the power of the written word.

You are deepening your relationship with the MOST important person in your life – YOU!

NOTE FROM THE COACH:

Dear You, I love you for recognizing that being a better you is important in how you feel while living your life. I love you for doing the activities that felt awkward. I love you for shifting perspectives, for releasing thoughts and beliefs that don't bring you JOY. I love you for doing your best to deepen your relationship with YOU.

Biography

Sheila is the single mother of two teens; a Daughter and a Son. She is passionate about her work in helping people get out of their 'story' because her journey to Happy, Healthy and Fulfilled stems from a *story* of her own.

Born into a family where both her parents were adult children of alcoholics; life as a child left Sheila feeling that safety, security and love were conditional. In order to feel validated and worthy she became a chronic *'people pleaser'* and that behavior continued on well into her late 30's. She was the *'perfect'* child, the *'perfect'* student, *'perfect'* employee. She also took her people pleasing behaviours and self limiting beliefs into her marriage.

She became a mother for the first time at 28yrs old and then again at 30 when her and her husband decided to attempt having Sheila become a stay at home mother.

Time passed and as she raised her children, supported her mother (who suffered from mental illness) and her husband she completely lost herself.

Medicated for depression and anxiety herself; Sheila found herself at 38yrs of age weighing more than she had ever weighed and struggling to keep up appearances.

Sheila was called to WAKE UP to her life.

To do the work and change how she was living in a profound way. Her *wake up call* came in various forms of 'undoing'. Over a period of approximately 9 years; her father passed, her mother passed, she got off her medications, lost approximately 80lbs of weight, her marriage ended and rock bottom became the foundation she used to rebuild her now BEAUTIFUL LIFE.

Sheila is passionate about helping others learn how to get rid of the labels, beliefs and behaviors that no longer support their desire to THRIVE.

As a Life Coach and Spiritual Guide. She works with the Mind, Soul, Body and Spirit helping people heal from their past and step into the fullest potential of their future.

Sheila is a highly intuitive Coach, Hypnotherapist and Energy worker, living and practicing in Oakville Ontario.

Her goal is to help as many people as possible

WAKE UP and SHIFT!

You can find out more about Sheila's Coaching practice at www.sheilahill.ca

Acknowledgements

Personal photography by:

Zoom Into Life Photography
www.zoomintolife.com

Chapter Illustrations:

I give thanks to the unknown photographers who willingly give their art for free so people like me who LOVE to play can use them to make beautiful creations.

5 Love Languages Test:

Taken from the teaching in the book:

"The 5 Love Languages"   by Gary Chapman

Editing:

Thank you so much my beautiful friend:
Barbara Chapman for her time, love and editing skills.

Graphic Design (Cover):

Thank you to Juana Iturriaga, graphic designer and friend.   www.hyperjane.com